Wind Energy

Wind Energy

Graham Morgan

Living in THE FUTURE

CREATIVE EDUCATION

CREATIVE PAPERBACKS

Published by Creative Education and Creative Paperbacks
P.O. Box 227, Mankato, Minnesota 56002
Creative Education and Creative Paperbacks are imprints
of The Creative Company
www.thecreativecompany.us

Book design by Blue Design (www.bluedes.com)
Art direction by Graham Morgan
Edited by Barbara Ciletti

Photographs by Alamy Stock Photo/peace portal photo, 32; Getty Images/Ashley Cooper, 29, cofotoisme, 10, Daniel Bosma, 26, NurPhoto, 41, Sergen Sezgin/Anadolu, 17; Pexels/Kervin Edward Lara, cover, Narcisa Aciko, 4–5, Pixabay, 9, 37, Quinten Sluis, 20, Songhan Wu, 14; Unsplash/American Public Power Association, 13, Fabian Wiktor, 43, Icaraizinho de Amontada, 44, Mathew Schwartz, cover, Nicholas Doherty, 31, Shinichiro Ichimura, 2, Thomas Richter, 6–7; Wikimedia Commons/Dat doris, 21, ENERGY.GOV, 25, Internet Archive Book Images, 19, NASA, 35, public domain, 23, Thepointstoryline, 38, Tobi Kellner, 45

Library of Congress Cataloging-in-Publication Data
Names: Morgan, Graham (Children's author) author
Title: Wind energy / by: Graham Morgan.
Description: Mankato, Minnesota : Creative Education and Creative Paperbacks, [2026] | Series: Living in the future | Includes bibliographical references and index. | Audience: Ages 10-14 | Audience: Grades 7-9 | Summary: "Explore the technology of wind turbines and how wind is used to generate electricity. This book highlights the potential of wind power in creating a cleaner energy future. Written for middle-grade readers, it includes real-life examples of energy use, sidebars, a glossary, and an index"— Provided by publisher.
Identifiers: LCCN 2025021633 (print) | LCCN 2025021634 (ebook) | ISBN 9798895811252 library binding | ISBN 9798896800781 paperback | ISBN 9798895812518 ebook
Subjects: LCSH: Wind power—Juvenile literature
Classification: LCC TJ820 .M675 2026 (print) | LCC TJ820 (ebook) | DDC 621.31/2136—dc23/eng/20250814
LC record available at https://lccn.loc.gov/2025021633
LC ebook record available at https://lccn.loc.gov/2025021634

Printed in the United States

CONTENTS

A Long History

Human beings have long been captivated by the invisible power of the wind, often thinking of it as a divine force. Many ancient cultures believed the wind was a living power connected to nature's order. In India and ancient Persia, sacred texts praised the wind as an essential part of life, often linking it to powerful deities. In Greek and Roman traditions, the wind took on human form through gods who commanded the skies. While many old stories might embellish or humanize the strength of the wind, our respect for it's power has remained steady throughout the millennia, and our ability to harness that power now fuels our everyday life. Wind **turbines**, now a common sight on hills and plains, show how far we've come in our ability to draw power from one of nature's oldest forces.

Real-time sensors continuously monitor turbine performance, wind, and mechanical health.

CHAPTER 1:

How Does Wind Energy Work?

Energy is central to human civilization. Modern society requires vast amounts of energy to function, and we have built enormous, complex systems to generate and distribute that energy.

Continent-spanning networks of power lines connect our cities, homes, hospitals, and schools. Thousands of miles of roads carry millions of cars and trucks. Trains, airplanes and cargo ships crisscross the world. Our energy network runs largely on **fossil fuels** such as coal, oil, and gas. But these fuels are expensive, polluting, and contribute to **global warming**—and they will eventually be used up. It is increasingly important to find **renewable** and **sustainable** alternative energy sources, including solar, hydropower, geothermal, nuclear power, biofuels, and the topic of this book, wind power.

Wind is a powerful natural force driven by Earth's rotation, air pressure shifts, and the sun's heat. And for thousands of years, humans have found ingenious ways to put it to use. Long before electricity, wind guided ancient ships across the seas and spun the blades of medieval **windmills** to grind grain or pump water. Today, wind has moved into the spotlight as a major source of clean, renewable energy.

Modern wind turbines are advanced machines designed to turn the natural movement of the wind into usable electricity. When the wind blows, it pushes against the long blades of the turbine, causing them to spin. These blades are shaped to catch the wind efficiently, much like an airplane wing. They are attached to a hub, which is part of a larger rotating piece called the **rotor**. As the rotor spins, it turns a central shaft inside the turbine. This shaft runs into a gearbox that increases the speed of rotation, since the blades spin relatively slowly. The fast-spinning shaft then drives a generator.

Inside the generator, a process called **electromagnetic induction** takes place. This means that as magnets spin around coils of wire, they cause electrons to move, creating an electric current. That current is the electricity we use in our daily lives. It travels down through cables inside the turbine tower and is sent to a transformer, which adjusts the voltage so it can be sent out through power lines. In simple terms, the energy from the moving wind is captured by the blades and

Wind energy creates no pollution during use, making it one of the cleanest power sources.

ZOOM IN: GREEN GOALS

To replace fossil fuels, alternative energy must be renewable, sustainable, and carbon-neutral. This means it won't run out, won't harm the environment or future energy use, and won't add extra carbon to the atmosphere. Wind energy meets all three standards, with only minor emissions from making and installing turbines. Overall, it's a clean and lasting energy source.

transformed into electrical energy that powers homes, schools, businesses, and even entire cities.

The amount of electricity a turbine can generate depends on how fast and steady the wind is. That's why wind farms are usually built in open areas where wind is strong and doesn't get blocked by trees or buildings. There are two main types of wind farms: onshore and offshore. Onshore wind farms are built on land and are easier and cheaper to install and maintain. Offshore wind farms are built out in oceans or large lakes. These turbines often produce more energy because the wind over water is usually stronger and more constant. However, offshore turbines are more expensive to build and harder to maintain due to their remote locations and harsh marine environments.

Wind now plays a key role for countries fighting climate change and driving the shift to cleaner energy. Land-based wind farms provide power that keeps lights on in homes, businesses, and factories. Ocean based wind farms produce large amounts of electricity by tapping into the powerful ocean winds. Smaller turbines provide off-grid energy to remote communities, and hybrid systems combine wind with other renewable sources to keep energy flowing smoothly.

There are plenty of reasons to love wind power. It doesn't release greenhouse gases or pollution while it's running. The "fuel" is free and never runs out. And once a turbine is up and spinning, the operating costs are low. Wind energy also creates thousands of jobs, from building turbines to keeping them running, and landowners can even lease space for turbines while still farming or raising livestock.

Beyond the technology and numbers, wind energy is able to bring people together. It empowers small communities to generate their own electricity, reduce their energy bills, and become more resilient. In some regions, wind projects are owned cooperatively by residents who share in the benefits. Schools and local organizations use wind energy projects to educate the next generation about science, sustainability, and **innovation**.

Of course, like any energy source, wind isn't perfect. It's dependent on the weather, some days are windier than others after all. However, advances in battery storage and smart grid technology are helping solve that. Turbines can also affect birds and bats, though new designs aim to reduce those risks. Some people have concerns about how turbines look or sound, and the upfront costs of building wind farms can be high. Even so, the technology keeps improving.

ZOOM IN: WATT DO YOU MEAN?

Energy use is commonly measured in watts, which indicate the power needed to do a task—a 40-watt lightbulb, for example, uses 40 watts of electricity to shine. Power stations, however, measure output in watt-hours, showing the total energy produced over time. One megawatt-hour (MWh) equals one million watt-hours, and one terawatt-hour (TWh) equals one million megawatt-hours. In 2023, wind energy generated over 2,000 terawatt-hours of electricity globally.

Hollow turbines hold electrical wiring, ladders and maintenance access.

The evolution of wind power is happening rapidly. Floating turbines are being developed to capture strong winds out in deep waters where fixed turbines can't reach. Energy storage solutions are becoming more sophisticated, helping balance out the ups and downs of wind production. With supportive policies and growing international commitments to cut carbon emissions, wind is expected to play a big role in powering our future.

People around 4000 BCE Used reed boats to sail the Nile and later developed larger ships for trade in the Red Sea and Mediterranean.

CHAPTER 2:

A History of Wind Power

Humans have been fascinated by the power of the wind for thousands of years. Long before modern turbines transformed breezes into megawatts of electricity, ancient peoples found ingenious methods to harness the invisible force of nature.

Thousands of years ago, ancient societies found ingenious ways to harness nature's forces. Early sailors captured the wind using sails to navigate the oceans, connecting distant cultures through trade. In China, engineers devised wind-powered pumps to draw water for crops, early proof that wind could do more than move ships; it could perform vital work on land.

By 200 B.C.E., both China and the Middle East had independently developed wind-driven machines to irrigate farmland and grind grain, crucial innovations that sustained daily life. These early inventions were mixed into daily life and reflected a growing mastery of environmental forces.

A significant leap in our adaptation of wind energy came with the emergence of the windmill. Between the 9th and 11th centuries, regions like

ZOOM IN: ANCIENT WINDMILLS

The first recorded windmills emerged in 9th-century Persia, known as **panemone** windmills for their vertical-axis design—wooden sails arranged around a central shaft captured the wind's energy to perform practical tasks. Initially, these early machines were used primarily to pump water for irrigation and to grind grain, which was vital for agricultural communities in arid regions. As the technology spread beyond Persia, it began to evolve to meet local needs and eventually gave rise to the iconic European windmills that many associate with rural progress and ingenuity.

Persia, Afghanistan, and Pakistan witnessed the development of the vertical-axis windmill. These early windmills, often made of sun-dried bricks or wood, harnessed wind power to grind grain and press oil. In Persia, for example, the windmill became an indispensable tool in **arid** regions where water was scarce but the wind was plentiful. This adaptation not only improved agricultural productivity but also spurred a cross-cultural exchange of wind technologies across the Islamic world and into Europe.

The **migration** of windmill technology transformed Europe. Medieval peoples quickly adopted and refined this technology, with windmills becoming symbols of rural prosperity. In the Netherlands, these windmills were essential for draining lakes and marshes. Wind power turned large wooden gears connected to a scoop wheel or screw mechanism. These lifted water from low-lying areas into canals or rivers at higher elevation, making the land suitable for farming and settlement. By converting wind energy into mechanical work, farmers could also more efficiently process grain and manage water supplies. This period revealed the many possible applications of wind power, laying a foundation that would support centuries of further technological evolution.

One of the pioneering moments in modern wind power history occurred in 1883 at the Vienna International Electrical Exhibition. Austrian engineer Josef Friedländer demonstrated a wind turbine designed to generate electricity. Friedländer's machine, though primitive by today's standards, represented a bold step toward integrating wind energy with emerging electrical networks. Soon after, other inventors in Europe and America took note, spurring a series of experiments that gradually refined wind turbine design .

Across the Atlantic, Scottish innovator James Blyth made his mark in 1887 by installing a cloth-sailed wind turbine in his garden at Marykirk, Kincardineshire. Blyth's turbine charged batteries that powered his holiday cottage's lighting. This was one of the first times wind power was used to give electricity to a home. Blyth's invention proved that wind could be a practical source of energy, especially for people living in places without easy access to the growing power grid. Blyth's work demonstrated the promise of wind energy in a modernizing world and inspired further ventures into wind-powered electricity.

Meanwhile, back in America, industrialist Charles Brush was busy. In Cleveland, Ohio, Brush constructed a larger wind turbine during the winter of 1887–1888. Mounted on an 18-meter tower with a rotor spanning 17 meters, his windmill represented one of the first instances of wind-generated electricity used to power not only lighting but also a range of household and laboratory equipment. Brush's system, although mechanically complex and modest

Charles Brush's wind turbine

in power output by today's metrics, was a crucial demonstration of how wind energy could be engineered to serve practical, everyday electrical needs.

In the mid 1920s, brothers Joe Jacobs and Marcellus Jacobs opened a factory called Jacobs Wind in order to produce wind turbine generators for farm use. By the 1930s, windmills were widely used to generate electricity on farms in the United States that were out of reach of central-station electricity and distribution lines. These windmills would typically be used for lighting or battery charging.

ZOOM IN: SAVE IT FOR LATER

Generating electricity from wind is challenging, but storing that energy adds another layer of difficulty. Wind is unpredictable, it can be strong one moment and completely calm the next. That's why energy storage is so important. While we're familiar with everyday batteries, energy storage also includes bigger systems. For example, some wind farms use extra electricity to pump water uphill into a reservoir, then release it to produce power when needed. Others compress air in underground spaces to use later. Scientists are even working on turning wind energy into fuels like hydrogen to help create a more reliable, renewable energy system.

Even though wind power had some early successes, it didn't immediately change the way electricity was made and used. In the late 1930s, as programs brought electricity to more rural areas, like in the United States, big power plants and long-distance power lines became more common. Because of this, small wind generators on farms and ranches were used less and less. Still, in far-off places without access to power grids, wind pumps remained important. They helped supply water and supported basic needs, showing that wind was still a dependable source of energy in remote areas during a time of big changes.

A Jacob's Wind windmill, commonly used on rural farms in the United States.

People began to rethink their approach to renewable energy. In the 1970s, the world faced oil shortages that caused major economic problems. These events pushed countries to look for new sources of energy. Wind power got more attention as a clean and renewable option. Governments began funding research to improve wind technology. In the U.S., new laws and programs encouraged the building of wind turbines, especially in places with strong winds like California. These early wind farms showed that wind energy could work on a large scale and help reduce the use of fossil fuels.

Throughout the 1980s and 1990s, wind power technology underwent significant refinement. Advances in aerodynamics, materials science, and electrical engineering transformed wind turbines

into efficient, reliable sources of renewable electricity. The increased understanding of wind dynamics led to the design of blades that could capture energy more effectively, and innovations in gearboxes and converters made it possible to integrate wind-generated electricity into national grids. During this period, wind energy went from being a niche application to a competitive component of the global energy mix.

Today, wind power plays a growing and vital role in the world's energy system. Wind farms, which include groups of wind turbines, can now be found in many places around the world—both on land and offshore. The technology behand these turbines has improved a lot over the years. They have become more efficient, more reliable, and better able to handle changing wind speeds. Engineers use modern control systems to help turbines adjust their performance depending on the weather and wind conditions.

Wind power combines well with with other renewable energy sources like solar and hydropower. Working together, these sources help make the power grid more stable and flexible, especially when one source isn't producing as much energy. As the world looks for cleaner energy options and tries to cut down on pollution from fossil fuels, wind energy is expected to become even more important.

Researchers are preparing for the future by working on new turbine designs that can be used in deeper waters, such as floating offshore turbines. They are also improving blade materials so they can last longer and perform better in rough weather. While wind power isn't a perfect solution to the world's energy problems, it is becoming a more reliable and important part of how electricity is made in our modern world.

Hybrid systems combine solar and wind energy for a more stable, efficient power supply.

CHAPTER 3:

Wind Energy Today

Although the United States has held its reputation as a leader in wind energy innovation for a long time, the last two decades have witnessed changes in the global wind landscape. While America continues to grow their strong wind energy sector, nations across Europe and Asia have surged ahead, building larger and more complicated wind farms.

Countries around the world are investing in wind power, and enormous progress is being made. In 2023, the total amount of wind energy installed globally passed one terawatt—a major achievement after years of growth. China is leading the way, with more wind power than any other country. It has over 441,000 megawatt-hours (MWh) of wind capacity, far more than the United States, which has about 148,000 MWh. China's success comes from strong government support, smart investments, and good locations for wind. In fact, almost half of all the wind power in the world is now in China.

Moving massive components is one of the most difficult parts of turbine construction.

ZOOM IN: OFFSHORE POWER

Offshore wind farms are groups of wind turbines built out in the ocean to capture the strong, steady winds found over water. These winds tend to be more consistent than those on land, which means offshore wind farms can generate lots of clean electricity. The turbines stand on specially designed structures that can handle harsh sea conditions, like strong waves and salty water. Once the turbines convert wind energy into electricity, underwater cables carry the power back to the shore, where it is fed into the local power grid.

Wind power remains a vital part of the United State's energy grid. In many regions, wind energy accounts for a significant percentage of power generation. In states such as Texas, wind farms have transformed vast open spaces into clusters of modern turbines, contributing up to 20 percent or more of local electricity demand during optimal wind conditions. Other states such as Iowa and Oklahoma, with their abundant wind and flat terrain, contribute substantially to the nation's renewable energy. In fact, wind energy's share in the overall U.S. electricity mix has steadily grown over the past few years, reinforcing its role in **diversifying** the nation's energy sources. Market investments in wind projects and related engineering innovations have expanded remarkably, which has in turn created incentives for both private and public sectors to drive further growth.

Like hydropower, wind energy depends a lot on location. The best places for wind power are areas with steady, strong winds like wide open plains, coastlines, or out at sea. In the U.S., the Great Plains and the Atlantic and Pacific coasts are especially good for wind energy. But in places where the wind is less reliable, it helps to combine wind with other renewable sources or use energy storage to keep power flowing. Seasons also matter. In many areas,

Offshore wind farms generate more energy than onshore wind farms, however they have higher construction and maintenance costs.

ZOOM IN: SOUTHERNMOST ENERGY PROJECT

The Ross Island Wind Farm is the southernmost renewable energy project in the world, located on Crater Hill, Ross Island in Antarctica. Consisting of three turbines, it provides power to New Zealand's Scott Base and the US's McMurdo Station. It was built to reduce reliance on diesel fuel and cut greenhouse gas emissions by harnessing strong winds in one of the few ice-free areas on the island. Constructed during the Antarctic summer, it serves as a remarkable example of adapting modern wind technology to one of the planet's harshest environments.

wind is stronger during colder months, which is helpful because that's when people use more energy for heat and electricity.

Wind energy is now a major part of Europe's clean energy plan. Countries like Denmark, Germany, and the United Kingdom are leading the way with both onshore and ocean-based offshore wind farms. Denmark, for example, gets more than 40% of its electricity from offshore wind. Germany has built many wind turbines along its northern coast, and the Netherlands is creating advanced offshore wind platforms. These countries also use energy storage and smart grid systems to make sure power stays steady, even when the wind changes.

In Asia, wind energy is growing even faster. In 2023, China added over 70 gigawatts of new wind power—more than 75% of all new wind energy built that year. China's wind farms are huge, both on land and out at sea, and are built quickly using the latest technology. India is also expanding its wind power, especially in its wide rural and coastal areas, with help from government programs and new technology. Together, countries in Europe and Asia are changing how the world uses wind energy—producing clean power, creating jobs, and pushing the technology forward.

There are challenges of course. One of the main issues is that wind doesn't blow steadily. Turbines work only when there's enough wind, so power output can vary significantly throughout the day and across different seasons. This inconsistency makes it difficult to predict how much energy will be produced at any given time and to balance supply with demand. To address this, grid operators have to rely on improved forecasting techniques and invest in energy storage systems like batteries, which help smooth out the changes in power production. Power grids also must be upgraded with smart technology to better handle energy from the wind when mixed with other power sources.

Building and running wind turbines comes with other challenges. One major issue is cost. Turbines need a lot of steel and special materials called **rare earth elements** to make strong magnets. As these materials get more expensive, so does building and maintaining wind farms. Wind turbines have many moving parts—like blades, gears, and control systems—that need regular maintenance, which adds to the cost and makes large wind farms harder to manage.

Environmental and community concerns also play a role. While wind energy is clean, some people worry about the noise, how wind farms look, and the effect on animals. That's why careful planning and working with local communities is crucial when choosing wind farm locations.

Even with these challenges, wind energy has a strong future. Governments in places like the European Union are setting big goals for renewable energy and investing in offshore wind projects. In the U.S., both state and federal programs are helping modern wind farms grow and improving the energy grid. And in parts of South America, Africa, and the Middle East, new wind projects are starting, showing that clean wind energy is becoming a global solution.

Advanced imaging and atmospheric monitoring improve wind forecasting precision.

CHAPTER 4:

Looking to the Future

Wind energy has grown from an experiment to a vital part of renewable energy programs. A few decades ago, there were only a few large wind farms, but today, wind turbines, both on land and at sea, can be seen in many places around the world, ready to provide power to millions of people.

The journey of wind energy has been one of constant evolution. Early inventors harnessed the power of the wind with relatively simple designs, much like basic windmills on windy plains. Over time, advancements in turbine technology, materials science, and digital controls have propelled wind energy into a mature and increasingly reliable technology.

A single turbine can power 1,500 households per year.

ZOOM IN: ELECTROMAGNETIC INDUCTION

Why do turbines need magnets? When the wind turns the blades of a turbine, they spin a shaft connected to the generator. Inside the generator, magnets help convert that spinning motion into electricity. The magnets create a magnetic field, and as parts of the generator spin inside this field, they produce an electric current. This process is electromagnetic induction. Therefore, the magnets are key to turning the mechanical energy from the wind into usable electrical energy.

In 2024, planned wind power capacity around the world grew by over 20%, showing how important wind energy is for reaching a clean, net-zero future. Today's turbines have improved blade designs and smart control systems that make them work even better. The strong winds over the ocean mean that the development of offshore wind farms is especially exciting.

As wind technology grows, innovators are exploring ways to extract even more energy from the air. High-capacity turbines with longer blades and advanced materials now turn under lower wind speeds while generating large amounts of electricity. Floating wind turbine platforms are beginning to chart unknown waters—literally—allowing installations in deeper ocean locales where the winds are the most potent. Researchers are also investing in digital simulations and sensors that optimize turbine performance and predict maintenance needs, further improving the efficiency and reliability of wind farms. Urban wind turbines, along with other renewable energy systems working together, can help meet local power needs. At the same time, batteries are used with wind installations to keep the power supply steady when the wind isn't consistent.

While wind power is a clean alternative to fossil fuels, it does come with some environmental concerns. Studies show that when many wind turbines are built close together, they can reduce the number of insects in certain areas. This happens because the turbines can change the soil and plants, which insects rely on to survive.

Other research from Sweden has found that wind turbines can be dangerous for birds and bats, especially if they are built along migration routes. However, offshore wind farms might actually create new habitats for sea life, like artificial reefs that help marine animals. The impact of wind energy on nature is complicated.

It's important to choose turbine locations carefully and to design turbines with wildlife in mind. People in communities and conservation groups often debate how to balance building wind farms with protecting nature. Some suggest using technology like radar to detect birds and temporarily stop turbines during migration seasons. Others think wind projects should simply respect local environmental needs to keep both wildlife and people happy. Finding a balance between clean energy and

ZOOM IN: RADER DETECTION

Some wind farms use radar systems to help protect birds and bats from being harmed by turbine blades. These systems can detect when large flocks or individual animals are approaching. If a risk is spotted, the radar can trigger the turbines to slow down or temporarily stop, reducing the chance of collisions. This kind of technology helps balance the need for clean energy with efforts to protect local wildlife.

Wind turbine technicians—called windtechs—perform one of the most physically demanding and high-stakes jobs in the renewable energy field.

protecting the environment is a continuing challenge for wind power developers.

Climate change poses further challenges. As it changes weather patterns worldwide, wind energy is both a solution and something that needs **adaptation**. When temperature imbalances become more pronounced, wind currents may intensify, potentially boosting energy generation. Yet unpredictable shifts in wind patterns could pose operational challenges that require a new generation of agile, more data-driven turbines. This notion of being adaptable—of flowing like the wind itself—resonates with the renewable future, driving engineers and policymakers to make sure that wind energy systems can adjust to the inevitable uncertainties posed by a changing climate.

Climate change poses further challenges. As it changes weather patterns worldwide, wind energy is both a solution and something that needs adaptation.

In the quest for a fossil-fuel-free future, wind energy is poised to play an important role. It provides a sustainable, virtually pollution-free source of electricity harnessed from the breath of the planet.

With continued advancements in turbine technology, improved grid integration, and ongoing research into mitigating environmental impacts, wind energy looks set not only to maintain its present momentum but to expand into new territories. Future energy landscapes may be defined by a dynamic network of wind farms. Humans have long embraced the power of the wind, harnessing its boundless energy to better our society, and as we move forward into a more sustainable future, we´ll continue to let it chart our course.

Getting Real:

LOCATION

When selecting a location for wind turbines, there are many important factors that developers and engineers carefully evaluate to make sure the turbines work efficiently and don't cause unnecessary harm to the environment. One of the most important things to consider is wind speed and consistency. Turbines need strong, steady winds to produce electricity effectively, so areas that have reliable wind patterns—such as open plains, coastlines, hilltops, or ridges—are often ideal. In contrast, places like forests, valleys, or urban areas tend to have slower or more irregular winds because of physical obstructions like trees, buildings, or uneven land.

The shape and condition of the land also play a big role. Flat and open areas are easier to build on and allow for better wind flow, while rough or hilly terrain can make construction more difficult and reduce wind performance. Another major factor is how close the location is to the existing electrical grid. If a site is far from power lines, it can be very expensive and time-consuming to connect it to the grid. Choosing a location near existing infrastructure helps lower costs and improves the overall efficiency of the wind energy system.

Environmental impact also needs attention. Developers must study how turbines might affect local wildlife, especially birds and bats that could fly into the spinning blades.

Finally, weather patterns are examined in detail. Areas that experience extreme weather—like high winds, hurricanes, or heavy icing—may require special turbine designs or extra protection. All of these factors are studied carefully to choose the best locations for wind turbines, helping to make wind power safer, more reliable, and more environmentally friendly.

DO IT YOURSELF!

Using wind power at home involves setting up a small wind turbine that captures the energy of the wind and turns it into usable electricity. These turbines work by spinning when the wind blows, converting the wind's motion into electrical energy through a generator. For the system to be effective, the turbine needs to be installed in a location that gets strong, steady wind—ideally at speeds of at least 10 miles per hour. Open areas like hilltops, fields, or large backyards are best because there are fewer obstacles, such as tall trees or nearby buildings, that can block or slow down the wind.

The electricity the turbine creates is in the form of direct current (DC), which must be converted into alternating current (AC)—the type of electricity most household appliances use. This is done using a device called an inverter, which is a key part of the wind system setup. Many home wind power systems also include batteries, which store extra energy that can be used later when the wind is not blowing or when power needs are higher than usual. Some setups also connect to the local utility grid, allowing homeowners to use wind power when available and switch to grid power when necessary.

While a single home wind turbine might not be able to run everything in your house all the time, it can significantly reduce your energy bills. It also helps cut down on your use of fossil fuels and lowers your environmental impact. Over time, using wind power at home can contribute to a more sustainable lifestyle and even increase the energy independence of your household.

Timeline

1883

Austrian engineer Josef Friedländer builds one of the first wind turbines designed to generate electricity, marking an early step in modern wind power development.

1887

Scottish inventor James Blyth installs a wind turbine to power lights in his holiday cottage, demonstrating wind energy's potential for home use.

1930s

Rural electrification programs lead to centralized power grids in the U.S., causing a decline in small-scale wind generators on farms, though wind pumps remain important in remote areas.

1970s

The oil crises spark renewed interest in renewable energy worldwide, with governments supporting wind power research and development..

1980s

Commercial wind farms begin to appear in places like California

1990s

Advances in turbine design, materials, and grid integration transform wind energy into a reliable part of the global energy mix.

2000

The global installed wind power capacity reaches 17,000 megawatts (MW)

2010

Offshore wind farms start to expand

2023

Global installed wind power capacity surpasses 1 terawatt (1,000,000 MW), with China leading the market.

2024

Planned global wind power capacity grows by over 20%, signaling wind energy's increasing role in the shift toward sustainable electricity worldwide.

Websites

U.S. Department of Energy – Wind Energy Technologies Office
https://www.energy.gov/eere/wind
Offers detailed information on wind energy research, technology, and policy in the U.S.

World Wind Energy Association (WWEA)
https://wwindea.org
International organization providing info on wind energy advocacy and development.

Glossary

adaptation—the process of adjusting to new conditions, like changes in climate or technology, to better handle challenges

arid—a dry area with little rainfall, often having limited plant and animal life

diversifying—adding different types or varieties to make something more varied or balanced, like using different energy sources

electromagnetic induction—The process of generting electricity by moving a magnet near a coil of wire, which creates an electric current

fossil fuels—Natural energy sources like coal, oil, and natural gas formed from ancient plants and animals buried underground

global warming—a person who comes to live permanently in a foreign country; a foreign-born residenti

innovation—the creation of new ideas, methods, or inventions to solve problems or improve things

migration—the spread or movement of something from one place to another

net-zero—Balancing the amount of greenhouse gases emitted with the amount removed from the atmosphere, resulting in no net increase.

panemone—– A type of vertical-axis windmill that utilizes wind drag to rotate a central shaft, typically featuring multiple sails arranged around the axis.

rare earth elements—A group of metals used in many modern technologies

rotor—A rotating part of an electrical or mechanical device

renewable—energy from sources that won't run out, like wind, solar, or water power

sustainable—using resources in a way that meets current needs without harming the ability of future generations to meet theirs.

turbines—machines that spin when wind, water, or steam moves them, turning that motion into energy like electricity

windmills—older machines that use wind power to grind grain or pump water, often with large blades turning around

Selected Bibliography

Chiras, Dan. *Power from the Wind: Achieving Energy Independence.* Gabriola Island, BC: New Society Publishers, 2009.

Mattern, Joanne. Catching the Wind: *The Story of Wind Energy.* New York: Scholastic Inc., 2017.

Manwell, James F., Jon G. McGowan, and Anthony L. Rogers. *Wind Energy Explained: Theory, Design and Application.* Chichester, UK: Wiley, 2009.

Righter, Robert W. *Wind Energy in America: A History.* Norman: University of Oklahoma Press, 1996.

Index